THE
PROPHECY
OF
CHRISTOS

THE
PROPHECY
OF
CHRISTOS

Michael Blackburn

JACKSON'S ARM
Lincoln

Acknowledgements are due to the editors of the following: *La Carta de Oliver* (Argentina), *Foolscap, Panoply (USA), Poetry & Audience, Scratch, Slow Dancer, Smoke, Tees Valley Writer, The Wide Skirt: Images for Africa* (WaterAid, 1988) and *High on the Walls* (Morden Tower/Bloodaxe Books, 1990). Other poems are drawn from the following collections: *The Constitution of Things* (Northern House, 1984), *Why Should Anyone Be Here And Singing?* (Echo Room Press, 1987) and *The Lean Man Shaving* (Jackson's Arm, 1988).

© Michael Blackburn 1992
ISBN 0 948282 09 6

first published 1992 by
JACKSON'S ARM
P.O. Box 74
Lincoln LN1 1QG
England

cover: Geoffrey Mark Matthews
typography: John Wardle

CONTENTS

The Constitution of Things, 7
Elegy, 8
Motorway Birds, 9
1918: Letter from Moscow, 10
Gulliver's Lilliput, 11
Light and Rain, 12
Tutankhamen's Antechamber, 13
Seaford, 14
In Memoriam A. Beck, 15
Chalet, 16
Simple Things, 17
The North Sea at Tynemouth, 19
E.C.T., 20
Why Should Anyone be Here And Singing?
1. Purple Safari Dawns, 21
2. Free Market Economy, 22
3. Movie-City, 23
4. Neighbours in Soho, 24
5. Flirtation '81, 25
6. Aerial Surveillance, 26
7. One More, 27
8. Danny's Departure, 28
9. Harry to Jack in the Underground, 29
10. Reckoning, 30
11. The Days in Between, 31
The Lean Man Shaving, 32
The Garden Enclosed, 33
The Lodger, 34
Grey, 35
Exercise, 36
Regimental Association Dinner Dance, 37
Soldiers on Exercise, 38
Stories from the Park, 1916, 39
Czech Family Photos in a London Junkshop, 41
From the Black Cuillin Peaks, 42

Icarus,   43
Lead,   44
That Ship,   45
Debt,   46
Crocodiles,   47
The Sentimental Man Considers Snow,   48
Albion's Poverty Tree,   49
Tearing,   50
A Suitcase Full of Old Love Letters,   51
A Nuclear Family,   52
The Forgotten,   54
Cragside,   55
The Prophecy of Christos,   56
Water,   57

THE CONSTITUTION OF THINGS

Conspiracy of spaces
                tautened with energies.
It could just happen
that I walk straight through a wall
or put my hand through a table.

Then we may all be ghosts.

One day the apple will not fall
but hang in the air below my hand.

ELEGY

spat out each day
his green phlegm, for the sea
crept in his lungs
ships all this time
sliding from the rivermouth
their foghorns along the coast
waking the sea

and he too went graveward
weary of his body-house
sea growing wide in his chest

MOTORWAY BIRDS

rooks black companions
of torn rubber cast
along the lay-bys
untidy with wind-
wrenched feathers flap down
to noise-level where
people emerge from cars

kestrels quivering dip
slide the balance of wind
pin out the green line
of their motorway, eyes
focus down pick off
minute warm traffic of
mice and voles

1918: LETTER FROM MOSCOW

'remember the things that Anton's mother
used to pile upon the table, pastries
and duck and fruit?

now everyone eats dogs and horses
we have a new administration

my hair is very white

I wish Anton were alive'

GULLIVER'S LILLIPUT

At first they sewed me to the earth
with a million threads.

Later, I took their fleets, to stop a war.
I pissed on their burning palace.

Back home, life is not the same.

LIGHT AND RAIN

In the spray behind cars and wagons
rainbows shifted, half-formed. Light,
cutting down from ledges of cloud,
shattered neatly through prisms of fine rain,
spanning two arcs across the motorway.

We drove through a pummelling wind,
the driver talking only of floods in the west.

Those brief elemental bridges hung
always before us, impassable.
Behind us in our spray we churned
prisms for those who followed.

TUTANKHAMEN'S ANTECHAMBER

Cluttered, a child's room,
wicker chairs, boxes,
wooden animals of many colours
and four chariots inlaid
with gold, glass and precious stones.

Wherever he's gone,
he's left all this behind.

SEAFORD

For Sarah
look where the tide has dropped
scores of white cuttlefish bones
to gleam on the stony shore

take these two to keep

as the sun sucks the ocean from them
their brackish memory will reek
till they're as clean of odour
as they are of flesh

I have a picture of you
leaning back on the seawall

a brittle white fragment in your fingers

IN MEMORIAM A. BECK

Our leaving cars crackle on the gravel drive
and the rooks' tall trees
shudder in the chill.

It was not long ago
you walked the dogs in the new snow.

There is no news now.

CHALET

out on the dark sea
the buoy's light flicked
on and off

its bell struck
with each long swell

in the chalet on the
clay cliff, grey fossils
from the beach
now in my pocket, I
passed the door of the room
where my young cousin slept

and as the bell
struck and the light
flicked I heard him
whimper from time to time

SIMPLE THINGS

1.

such simple things appear
to remind us –

a single strand of hair
entwined in a shoelace

such simple things appear;
nothing stronger than a hair

2.

April: England and Africa

Africa's heat makes roads
tremble and melt. You travel
with someone else, stepping from his
land-rover in dusty village streets
to buy oranges. The people
stare at your white beauty.

Wet with the morning's snow
the pear tree is in flower
at the bottom of my cool garden.

3.

When She Sleeps

a quiver of warm limbs
a delicate stillness

asleep now, she is
all her own

and when she moves
she does not know
which way she turns

4.

the window streamed with rain
and the rain stripped the lilac
by the wall

when you came back from the empty house
you stood by the door
the rain tasted sweet on your mouth

5.

her fingers trace patterns
in the dust on a walnut table

her pressed and silent lips make
no secret of her wish to leave

it was not always like this

THE NORTH SEA AT TYNEMOUTH

The sea folds over upon itself
again and again,
sucks and chews the shore
till rocks become sand.

Ships ride along its back.
Sometimes the water invades them
and they drown.

Darkness begins only
a couple of feet below,
extending through acres of cold compression
where the silver shoals graze.

Returning along the pier I watch
the pilot's boat greeting a visitor.
Surely they too have felt,
even on the stillest of days,
a sudden vertigo on the sea's heights?

E.C.T.

She convulses. Images
burn up, memories and words
flame away for good.

She falls back to a scorched land.

Wakefulness comes together in
fragments of light.
She crawls up to it
to a bed in a strange room.

She sees a chair and the clothes
on it, pale blue jeans
and a white shirt.
Her slow eyes track to a
cloudless window
then back to the chair again.

For a long time she stares,
unable to understand. She begins
to cry, not recognising
her own clothes.

WHY SHOULD ANYONE BE HERE AND SINGING?

1. PURPLE SAFARI DAWNS

Comfortable voices of the not-badly-off
come prancing out of my radio;
Mombasa nights, Nairobi days, the stable regimes
and purple safari dawns; giraffe and gazelle
shot with Nikon, Pentax, Ricoh.
Bitter with my empty pockets and hours
I let them pin maps on the walls of my brain,
imagine I stand by the wagon to watch
wildebeest and zebra grazing in the haze,
the slim girl with golden limbs shading her eyes
as she hands me the latest lightweight binoculars.
Adjusting the lens I see only the dead sand
of a million years; tall, slow-moving waves of it.
I turn to speak, but the comfortable people have gone.

2. FREE MARKET ECONOMY

astronaut shades reflecting doubles
the man steps off his motorbike 750 cc
creaks in black leather up to the room
good stuff this no dreck coke I can get you
speed anytime acid as well some old peyote
buttons or mescalin caps next week no sweat
need any smack bush I got plenty Scottish
homegrown lotsa seeds red leb too or oil
if you like or even some crack just give me the word
his cheek is pocked like a lunar tract
he plugs the gaps in the chemical market
leaving his clients dazed with new goods
the folded notes crackling between leather and skin

3. MOVIE-CITY

Don't stare at the moon, you'll start seeing ghosts –
movie-line advice I give to myself to no avail.
Through the wings of the urban twilight
I scuttle home, playing the one-line extra still.
Perhaps next week the major part will arrive:
the call of the shops, new clothes, warm flat,
endless credit and three meals a day.
The moon's silver madness crackling in my blood
thrills like amphetamine hope. *It all began
in such an ordinary way* – the traction of work
to a populous place. Bad luck is just a zone
I'm passing through, where vampires snivel and twitch
and zombies dance like robots. One day I'll leave it
all behind in its *glimmer of putrescence*.

4. NEIGHBOURS IN SOHO

Accepting the Fat Man's free invitation
we enter a room where men sit alone,
washed blue by the light of screens.
The same naked actors in a tiny flat
play the same old story of hump, suck and jerk.
In black fishnet tights and leotard a woman
serves lager that's watery, warm and sour.
The Fat Man stares down your cleavage,
talking of parties at his country house.
He offers you work in his bar. You refuse.
The music continues while the films are changed
and the leotard woman has loaded the tray.
She's walking to a door beside the screens,
to a room where there's no free entry.

5. FLIRTATION '81

Ister, Hister, she says, the girl in black
whose message is eyeball sex, flirting in bars
with hoi polloi of the student classes
impressed with her knowledge of Nostradamus.
She's forgotten Harry's name but he doesn't care,
lost in loss and bitter; Thames is Lethe
for all he knows, carrying condoms and corpses
to the Isle of Dogs. *Apocalypse,* she mutters,
and the boys around her shudder with lust,
each a marine with a megaton desire
predestined to implode in frustration.
Harry's away in the blue basement of a dream,
watching a sea without walls from a beach of blue sand
where a ticker-tape snickers the single word, *war*.

6. AERIAL SURVEILLANCE

These helicopter charms delight
only the fans of authority,
who want for nothing
and are not observed.
Ministers are high,
drafting laws to free
factories from their workers
and workers from their jobs.
The chopper strays from its river course,
its video bulge scanning
council estate and rented sector,
while DJs kowtow to royalty,
their common contempt for the populace
cooking the city like a microwave.

7. ONE MORE

one more rush of wind on a crowded platform,
one more drunk asleep on a bench,
one more nutter with a blitzed brain screaming,
one more smashed-up telephone, one more night of sirens,
one more ruck of skins shouting *kill the niggers*,
one more stranger's malevolent stare,
one more room at a criminal rent, one more landlord
trying it on, one more late train not arriving,
one more barman passing short change, one more
middle-class pig pushing in with his girlfriend,
one more pimp giving a Soho wink, one more pervert
buying in flashcubes, one more corpse for the river police,
one more trip to the social, one more time

8. DANNY'S DEPARTURE

When the lines move to collapse
there's no one there to help you
hold the broken ridgepole up.
You smile in the bar,
delirious as the rest of them,
the savage green spring
pushing you aside
like a stranger from yourself.
A house you can't inhabit;
it's all you can do
to pay the rent and leave
your keys on the kitchen table:
three-day jetsam
in the Beachy Head foam.

9. HARRY TO JACK IN THE UNDERGROUND

Jack, you're bringing me down
with all your pointless stories,
this endless drive
round the circuit of grief
in your scarred prophetic car.
All I want is to stay in one place,
to sleep a hundred years
and never dream once
of parties, pills and ecstasy.
The car's off the road, Jack,
the angels are truly tired.
They'll not rise to your summons,
fat old man rushing underground,
lonely as America.

10. RECKONING

Fate's tallyman totting up your indiscretions
is calling in your debts. You thought
your credit was good for a long time yet
but there's no way round with explanations –
lipstick stains on coffee-cups,
those scratchmarks on your back.
Everything's been so sweet, like the green
grapes you bought one morning
from a stall outside the tube. Her birthday.
You found a brown leaf the size of two large hands
to give her as a gift. She kept it,
moist with handcream, on her bedside table.
Now you remember her fine soft hair, the odour
of her leather jacket; and there's nothing you can say.

11. THE DAYS IN BETWEEN

I know the days in between; awake
to a morning like this, the city's breath
dusting my sill with monoxides. On the stair,
nothing but mail for the previous tenants.
A day when I talk with no one but myself
and the man who sells me cigarettes.
I'm walking through white-walled streets
down to the banks where houseboats lodge
on the black naked back of the river's mud.
Dusty June, the river is low.
The heart endures the unbearable one more day,
its automatic thud of hope and collapse. Suddenly I taste
the flush of panic. Like metal. Like blood.

THE LEAN MAN SHAVING

These hungry looks would've
worried Caesar. That's no
porcine friend in the glass,
no pliant man.

I practise a vulpine smile.
My energy flows inward, abstracting,
storing up like brown fat
in dense, thin layers.
Time for nothing
beyond my own purpose.

Leaves shiver in the darkness,
prickling Caesar's scalp.
The unsheathing of knives
is what he heard.
Sideways on, conspirators
slim as blades, with a hunger
patience whets.

I could wish for more fat
on these angular jaws. Tight,
shiny skin cannot conceal
the restless bone beneath.

He'd seen the same things in the glass
when young, testing sharp canines
with a fingertip.
Caesar was a lean man, too.

THE GARDEN ENCLOSED

from a painting by David Jones

The postcard I would have sent you
stands on my bookshelf, years later,
its colours weak from doses of sun.
Their faces are together, his lips
against hers, while the geese go running
into the wood. Everything leans to the left
as if the painter had drawn them
with his head inclined. The girl's
stiff body bends away like the smooth
forked limbs of the trees.
In the park by the river you talked
of a prisoner's childhood. Here in the city
you'd be free at last. Months after,
this card in my hand and the words in my head
failing at bridges, I felt like a child
beaten and banished from a fruitful place.
You are not like her, I thought, the painted girl
half-resisting what's already embraced.
But from the other side of the river
you never phoned, seldom wrote.
Friends who saw you noticed a change,
the untidy flat, its air of burnt weed and alcohol.
Perhaps when the boy is gone the girl
picks up her blue discarded doll,
goes back to tending her private garden.
In the picture it's still the same summer,
the yellow flowers have just been plucked
and the geese run off in alarm.
These two were never like us.

THE LODGER

For eighteen months he remained
a series of sounds, the single
man upstairs who nobody knew, for whom
no letters arrived, nor friends.
His slow soft footsteps came and went
at quiet unattended moments.
Sometimes I heard a record
repeatedly played, a cowboy
lamenting a faithless wife.
Late at night he'd rearrange
table, chair and wardrobe
as if there'd been something wrong
the way he'd done it the week before.
Seasons passed in our treeless road;
his personal sounds became
as natural to me as birdsong,
traffic or the ticking of wood
that cools in the dark.
One spring morning police arrived.
For a day there was silence
until he returned. That night
the furniture scraped and banged
and the cowboy lamented endlessly,
louder than before.

GREY

Even when summer
drags off the slabbed clouds
a greyness remains.

Like tasteless gas vacancy expands
over workbench, yard and factory.
People trickle away
as if their minds also
were smeared with grey.

When I see them I recall
my forebears in this graceless
town, and my back
aches for them, enduring
under such low ceilings.

EXERCISE

Coming down from the high windy moors
we'd walked half-way through them
before we noticed. On either side of the road
they lay as if resting, rifles lowered, helmets
and uniforms sprouting the coarse grass and heather
which grew about them. Their blackened faces
barely regarded us as we passed between.

An officer stood by the radio man;
the tall, thin aerial twitched and swayed.
No one spoke or made a sound.

We held our silence till out of their circle.
Behind us they merged back into the earth,
in their stillness listening for a message
to strike the quivering twig, waiting for the moment
when, lifting their rifles and jumping up,
they'd begin again.

REGIMENTAL ASSOCIATION DINNER DANCE

Her uncle in armaments
delivers the main speech.
Like a smooth horse
his voice leaps lightly
across the moral ditches.

I wonder if he sleeps
well of a night, dreaming
of tanks and artillery.

He leads such an interesting life,
she says as we dance,
he gets to travel so much.

Thirty-three and single,
she's a nurse.
Her father's had commands
all over Europe.

She talks as the music plays,
her voice, too, like a pony,
trotting, trotting.

SOLDIERS ON EXERCISE

children play
   games of death
lying down
   to jump up again
but these
   whose forms
equipment distorts
   till even the tallest
runs dwarflike
   when there's no
refuge in *pax*
   scorch in the blast
that's not a breeze
   sliced by metal
harsher than grass
   lie down to rot
and never rise

STORIES FROM THE PARK, 1916

Not unhandsome, a petit-bourgeois
gentleman strolling in South Park,
he surveys the busy tennis-courts,
the pathways and the flowers.

These he converts into weekly prose,
pink paper cuttings in a small green folder.
War news blurs through the back
of glue-buckled pages:
RUSSIANS DESTROY AUSTRIAN WORKS
INEXORABLE PUSH OF THE ALLIES.

Cancer awaits the blow from a ball
rising too swiftly for his bat
one Sunday at a friendly match.

Surgeons will remove the rancid gut.
In exchange for another ten years
half a lifetime will fall away
till he lies in a column of print
flanked by Wesleyans and spiritualists.

The night he died, father said,
he kicked the bed to bits.

Today in sunshine he pauses
in front of the Austrian pines.
That unhappy land – he sees
the words already in print,
quelling the problem Trees
of the Enemy Nations.

No tree hardier, he mumbles,
catching a scent, as he thinks,
of the Alps: clean, fresh
and healthy; a place above all
for the sportsman, like himself.

CZECH FAMILY PHOTOS
IN A LONDON JUNKSHOP

Angular pastel designs streak the blackness
between photographs, drawn by a caring hand,
perhaps by one of the two young girls who appear
from one page to another, in long coats
and knee-length boots, smiling in a street
or on the steps of a building surrounded by snow.

They've come all the way from wartime Prague,
the girls who sat with their family at home
or picnicked by a stream where their dog, Kamerad,
swam with a stick in his mouth.

They make me see myself like them, four decades hence,
unnamed among my own people and places, when some
stranger in a dusty shop one afternoon, picking up
an album of pictures, tries to imagine
the voices, the looks, the domestic details.

The album's not full. It stops without a date
at a young man in uniform, his coat buttoned
tightly to the throat. He stands, straight and nameless,
in a field, alone. A black silence begins here
which no one has tried to fill. I close the book
and leave them to their privacy.

FROM THE BLACK CUILLIN PEAKS

The brittle rock holds up
its own dark nature, so full of friction
you feel you could climb
with naked fingers and feet
to the highest zone of attrition.

In this clean Hebridean light
extending through nameless blues
of sea and air, the burn has dwindled
to a thin white stillness, and from the soft
surrounding brown of its heather
cuckoos call.

Somewhere on a steep grey slope scree
tinkles and rolls from a walker's boot.
You tilt your head, abruptly aware,
gravity's hunger, under it all.

ICARUS

Earth is full of monsters
    so my father taught me
imprisoned in the tower.

I gulped the warm freedom of air
    a little too much, and the wax
dribbled on my arms.

Because the water loved me
    I gave my breath to it
sluicing its cool brine slowly

through chambers of heart and bone.
    I swivel on the sea-bed now
with wings too heavy to lift

and move at the prompting of tides
atom by atom my flesh unbonding.

LEAD

the buildings are demolished
or crumbling, powder-house
and smelting-mill
the long flues collapsing
up the hill

tic-ridden bracken
thickens to the water's edge

still I pick stones
like a child eager to find
unearthed ore
dusting the fingers
with its weighty presence

poison, said mother
wash your hands when you've touched it

the cool beck licks
my fingers clean
and does not die

THAT SHIP

You watch that ship from the certainty
of shore, far off, motionless perhaps,
or half-submerged under the future's rim.

Sometimes it will pass, cruising close by,
unexpectedly swift and easeful,
so close you can hear its engines and glimpse
shadowy still figures who stare and do not wave.

Who knows when the last stage begins,
one minute on shore then suddenly aboard,
watching land slide away, as if it were a dream,
heading for the unlimited sea?

DEBT

He stayed a year,
eating his pizzas off the fridge-top
because he wouldn't sit with the others.
In the morning he'd cheese the air
with yoga in the living-room.
He didn't like the girl, but she paid him no mind.
The other men ignored him.

After he left he sometimes called in,
carrying his black important briefcase.
He'd lay it on the floor,
thumbing its combination to reveal
the papers of his latest endeavour.

They began to forget him then one day found
his lost wallet down the side of a chair.
They disposed of it and any guilt they felt,
after they took the money.
He owed them, they reckoned,
for a year's unfriendliness;
surely a loss he'd already accepted.

CROCODILES

Quiet as linen folded in a cupboard,
calm as milk and steady as bread,
everything domestic – weighed and washed,
wrapped, capped and binned.

Then I shine a torch into every box, every
shelf of darkness, saying, *look, no crocodiles,*
to my daughter, who's been frightened
by a picture in a book.

Yesterday a woodlouse was a crocodile.
So was a worm, then a spider. *No,* I explained,
crocodiles are big, like this, stretching my arms
wide, like a fisherman.

But anything will do for a nightmare,
even a ladybird on the leg of a chair.
That's when love breaks in me, and plummets,
helpless as Niagara.

THE SENTIMENTAL MAN CONSIDERS SNOW

children love it
like a new toy
building their legless people
along the riverbank

when did I
cease to love it?

sometime in the city
its delicate arrival
turning to slush
on the road to work

ALBION'S POVERTY TREE

it roots in cellars of unread books
and ancient servitude

it splits the house,
the marriage bed, the nursery

envy and spite are its evergreen leaves
so tight its branches no light can pass through

its shade is hemlock
its trunk a black battering rod

see the roof explode
in a cloud of shrapnel messages

house after house, a brutal skyline

it will make a forest
it will eat the sun

TEARING

she's crying in the street
and won't let go
I can't hear their voices
but their hands become mouths
she grips him by the arm
or ties him by the neck
he takes each wrist and holds it up
and pushes her back
but she's like a spring
and keeps on returning
he's progressing slowly
a few feet backward each time
and she's losing him
and knows it
but can't stop
and the more she understands it
the greater her despair
and the more she cries for him
the further it drives him
and I can't watch any more of this
hurting for both of them

A SUITCASE FULL OF OLD LOVE LETTERS

Almost, that is. Almost all love letters
and almost full.

And photographs, the four-strips taken
drunkenly in machines outside the tube.
You with a cigarette, giving me *that look*;
us kissing, me swearing.

We look like someone else's children.

There are better ways to end than badly.
That's what I learned
from the days when I used to smoke.

A NUCLEAR FAMILY

in this one the father is weak *because of his breakdown*
and has hated the neighbours from the day they moved in
it's almost as if he isn't there any more he hardly talks
to the children two daughters dominated
by their ambitious mother who has pretensions
to class blaming *him* always *him* for whom she gave up
everything while he has just given up on their marriage
which has soured through every distillation
of disappointed status and sex though neither will
end it him because *it's not done* and he's too helpless
to look after himself her because she's
not strong enough to survive on her own not having had
work since the children and anyway for people
of their generation *it's simply not done*
so the children grow up in this cold warped climate
with the snapping songs of disenchantment in their heads
paying attention to etiquette and how the neighbours
think according to their parents' gospel and learning
nothing about love or honesty or warmth
and they get along fine till they argue over
a dress or a friend or something trivial in their teens
and don't speak to each other for five years
communicating via mother or father at the table
as if they were at a committee meeting
one of them envying the other for her looks
the other envious of her sister's intelligence
and mother looking on playing off one against the other
with *I'm not well again it's your father*
and her ill-health *he's so selfish you wouldn't*
believe it while he fades even further into
unimportance ignoring the wielding of guilt
like a cattle prod on his daughters

and as they grow she berates the younger
you're a failure just like your father comparing her
with the favourite who makes a success
out of money marriage and motherhood *how you
disappoint me* pursuing her like a fury
so she drifts drinks fails at this and that
tries a couple of suicides fails survives
dries out drifts on while she sees her sister
hardening to a salty pillar of stone like mother
always critical and condescending and her father
dried up to a grey silent ghost in his own household
*it's all his fault you don't know the half of it
the things he made me suffer* the litanies
of the self-damned jingling to the same tunes
so the years pass and she takes a trip back
to find one summer afternoon her mother
with a brush and a pot of paint drawing a white line
through the middle of the house across doorstep
lino carpet saying *he's done it now he's got what he wanted*
and pointing with the brush *that's his side of the house
this is mine he's not allowed on this side any more*
and she doesn't even say hello but carries on with her task
while her daughter bearing her thirty-three years
like a box of broken china walks away for the last time
without a word

THE FORGOTTEN

Spreti, your face comes back to me this autumn dawn
for no reason I can recall;
posthumous fame in the brevity of news,
you and your assassins, who saw the uniform
beneath the skin, that marked you as an enemy.

Still, this is the way of things;
news that is not news, while the trees
seal off their leaves and let them fall.

In a government office a typist cuts
her thumb on the edge of paper. She is
too young to remember your name, your face,
your fingers in a rigor about the broken
spectacles resting on your chest.

Leaves fall, numerous as memos.

There is no end to the freshness of victims.

CRAGSIDE

(Northumbrian country home of Armstrong, the Armaments King)

He dined on venison, pheasant, beef;
made a sweet microclimate for himself
with dynamite and a million trees.

See how tall they've grown –
spruce, larch, yew, sequoia –
from sloping shallows of acid soil.

No ghost steps from their shade to say,
Remember us who made his wealth
for nothing but a bent back and a short life.

In the kitchen cutlery is laid out for all to see:
knives and forks with big bone handles,
big enough for a giant.

A pine-cone, sealed up with all its seeds,
drops grenade-like to the needle-soft path.
The innocent trees, a century old,
still strive slowly toward the sun.

THE PROPHECY OF CHRISTOS

My future in the mud of a coffee-cup,
drying on a tissue:
children, divorce, work abroad.
It's like staring down a well of gold,
his wife translated.

He might as well have been poking a stick
in the guts of a chicken
or scanning the fractures
on a scorched rock.

When half is untrue, then what of the rest?

Sometimes I think it's either still to come,
or someone else has got my well of gold
and left me with the sludge of prophecy.

WATER

It changes things.
Just look at what the sea does
to pebbles and brick and fragments of glass.

Even the rock of this mountain before us
gets worn and worried by generations of rain.
Bit by bit the streams below
are carting it away to the sea.

The sea, as we know, has mountains of its own –
its briny work is never done.
Every day it sends more clouds
to remind us how things must change.